The History of Venezuela

A Fascinating Guide to

Venezuelan History

By

David Robbins

Table of Contents

Introduction

The Bolivarian Republic of Venezuela (or in Spanish, la República Bolivariana de Venezuela) is a medium-sized nation located in northern South America on the Caribbean Sea. It is bordered by Guyana, which is a former British Colony and Brazil and Colombia, which are both former Spanish colonies.

Twice the size of California, Venezuela is home to a large percentage of the world's oil reserves, which, when they were discovered, vaulted Venezuela onto the world stage. Despite that economic advantage, since its independence from the Spanish Crown in the early 1800s, Venezuela has spent most of its history in periods of political conflict.

The nation's economy and political life is centered on Caracas, which has been the capital of the nation since its sovereignty.

While the nation has undergone significant demographic changes, most notably during the Spanish invasions of South America during the 17th and 18th centuries, it is now home to people from a wide variety of ancestries, including Spanish, Italian, Portuguese, Arab, German, and African, along with a small percentage of indigenous people.

Spanish remains the official language of the Venezuela and it is estimated that 92-96% of the population practices Roman Catholicism, though the nation does not recognize an official religion. Both of these facts candidly demonstrate the continued influence of Spanish colonization of the country.

Venezuela also boasts one of the highest literacy rates in South America, with an estimated 93.4 percent of the population over the age of 15 able to read and write. There is a slight .7% discrepancy between the male and female literacy rates and Venezuela, while underfunded, continues to commit to providing free education for all its citizens.

Pre-Spanish

Before Venezuela, before the Spanish exploration, it is important to remember that there were indigenous people living within the modern day borders of Venezuela. The two best known of these groups are the Carib and Arawak Amerindian peoples.

Carib

You may first notice that the word "Carib" contains familiar letters. It is by no accident that the neighboring sea, the Caribbean, bears the same. Such is the influence of the Carib people. The word "Carib" also lent itself to English in the form of the word "cannibal" and the term "Cariban," which describes a group of related native languages spoken by the Carib people and many neighboring indigenous groups in South America.

Beyond their name, the Carib have had a significant impact on the people of the region. The Carib were divided into many groups across the region but it is thought that they originated from the islands of Carib, a grouping of lands in the Lesser Antilles, located between present day Venezuela and the Dominican Republic.

The Carib language was spoken only by the men while the women spoke Arawak. This divide may have contributed to a vast difference in gender roles. While the men were bellicose and aggressive—as noted by their many attacks on the Arawak people, driving them out of the region—the women were largely kept as slave-wives.

The groups of Carib that set their lives in the Lesser Antilles islands unsurprisingly spent much of their time on the water. They traveled in dugout canoes and took part in consistent raids of nearby civilizations. Successful exploits in battle were a primary part of a man's status within the people and, without a clear hierarchy, there was no sort of government within the Carib society.

In the mainland, the Carib were similar, but most groups were not quite so aggressive. They mostly lived south of the Amazon River and some sources claim they practiced cannibalism (this would explain the origin of the word cannibal into the English language).

While the Carib were widespread, they did not exhibit any sort of central government. Each group seemed to operate independently and, in fact, often fought with one another.

Arawek Amerindian

The Arawek people, while they lived in a similar region, were quite different than their Carib neighbors. The Arawek lived in villages of up to 3,000 people and focused their time primarily on agriculture. They were not warriors like the Carib and, as a result, were driven out of their ancestral homes in the Lesser Antilles soon before the Spanish arrived.

They were a greatly spiritual people, focusing on a hierarchy of nature spirits and ancestors that echoed their hierarchy of chiefs in their theocracy. Opposite of the Carib, the social organization amongst the Arawek was extremely complex for an early culture.

In addition to the Greater and Lesser Antilles, where they originated, the Arawek people spread across areas in the north and west of the Amazon basin and even reached the shadows of the Andes mountains. Those who left the islands had less social organization and hierarchy than their northern compatriots, but still focused primarily on agriculture.

Spain's Arrival

Like all South American people, the Carib and Arawak's way of life would be irrevocably changed by the Spanish Conquistadors.

The people in present day Venezuela, however, would be among the first to be affected. Christopher Columbus set foot in modern day Venezuela in 1498 in his third voyage to the new world. Shortly thereafter, Alonso de Ojeda and Amerigo Vespucci conducted explorations of the country with a wave of Spanish behind them. The land soon was named Venezuela because of the stilt houses on lakes that reminded explorers of Venice (Venezuela translates to "little Venice" in Spanish).

After Columbus landed in Venezuela, it took the Spanish about half a decade to found the land's first European cities. Valencia was the first, founded in 1555 in the central valley, surrounded by the Coastal Mountain Range. Soon after, in 1567, the Spanish founded Santiago de León de Caracas, the present day capital of Venezuela along the Guaire River and the Caracas Valley.

Both cities played a central part in the Spanish colonial economy, connecting Spanish sailing into the Caribbean to the whole of South America beyond Venezuela's borders. Those borders, however, operated quite differently than they do today. Instead of one country, colonial Venezuela operated more as five autonomous provinces: Caracas, Cumaná, Mérida de Maracaibo, Barinas, and Guyana. This autonomy was unique amongst South American colonies and led to interesting developments in Venezuelan culture.

Colonial Economics

Additionally, following the precedent of the Arawek people, agriculture—specifically cocoa— became the central economic activity in the colony. This allowed Caracas to grow quickly as its location made it the center of agricultural trade in the country. The inhabitants of the colony also grew wheat and tobacco and produced leather. None of these, unfortunately, were of much interest to the Spanish Crown. The Crown's quest was for gold, silver, and other precious metals to fund the famous Spanish Armada and a wide variety of foreign wars.

Venezuela, while a Spanish colony, made the bulk of its early money from other European countries, most notably Britain, France, and The Netherlands, despite frustration from the Spanish Crown.

As the cocoa market grew in the 17th century so did Venezuela. Spaniards flocked to the country, attracted by the growing possibility of making a fortune off the bean. This also led to a plantation culture reminiscent of the southern United States, leading to another market for the growing African slave trade.

Both the cocoa exports and the slave imports led to increased presence of British, French, and Dutch ships at Venezuelan ports. The Spanish Crown became frustrated with seeing a host of trade from their colony being sent to other countries and made a business move to solve the problem. In 1728, Real Companá Guipuzcoana de Caracas, written easier as the "Caracas Company," was given exclusive trading rights in Venezuela. Because the company was a Spanish one—located in the Basque region of Spain—this put Spain in de jure control of all trade in the colony.

At first, this seemed like a tremendously successful move by the Spanish crown. Profits skyrocketed, but dissatisfaction grew quickly amongst Venezuelan farmers. This largely contributed to a 1749 revolt led by Juan Fancisco de León, a working class farmer from the Canary Islands. Spain's forces were led by Brigadier General Felipe Ricardos, who made quick work of the revolt and as a result was chosen by the Crown in 1751 to become the next Governor of Caracas.

The revolt served to make Caracas even more central to the economy as the cocoa trade became completely centered around the city. The city was soon named the Captaincy General of Venezuela by Spain in 1777, effectively making Caracas the colonial capital and effectively naming Venezuela as a political entity.

This "power" given to the land by Spain would soon have a large effect on the unique population. By this time, the country was split into six clearly demarcated populations. On top of the social ladder were *peninsulares*, individuals born in Spain. They were closely followed by people born in Venezuela from Spanish parents, called *criollos*. After these two groups, a steep drop occurred to people from the Spanish-controlled Canary Islands—they were traditionally the paid working class of Venezuela—then the *pardos*, people who were mixes of all the groups. Below them were the African slaves brought in to provide cheap labor for agriculture and a severely reduced native population.

All of the above formed crucial economic functions to the burgeoning agricultural economy. The social elite—*the peninsulares and criollos*—formed the executive/administrative functions of the trade. They handled communication with the Spanish mainland and other nations interested in trading for the various agricultural products: primarily cocoa. They also oversaw the working class to ensure productivity.

The pardos and Canary Islanders formed the middle management layer as well as some of the labor force to ensure execution of the administrative and executive functions, and keep the laborers accountable.

Like any slave economy, the slaves formed the foundation of the economy. Without them productivity in Venezuela would have been impossible at the time. They grew and harvested the crops, forming the backbone of the agricultural economy.

Transition to Independence

After being named a General Captaincy, Venezuela continued to grow. By 1786, the entity had been named the Audiencia de Venezuela. This gave Venezuela authority of a large portion of its internal government affairs, including its judicial system.

It would not be long until the whole of South America was experiencing the beginnings of independence fever. This was soon aided by events in Europe as Napoleon came to power in France and began a wide variety of foreign wars throughout the world. The most relevant of these to Venezuela was the Peninsular War in which Napoleon overcame British, Spanish, and Portuguese opponents from 1808-1814.

With the Spanish Crown's focus on resisting Napoleon, its South American colonies would be left to fend for themselves. In many cases, Venezuela included, this gave many colonists the thought that they would be better off governing themselves and were not reliant upon Spain's support.

Colombia was the first South American to declare Independence from Spain, done so on July 20, 1810. Chile followed a few months after, then Paraguay, then Venezuela in 1811.

Like all of these declarations of independence, Venezuela's is not quite clear cut. The first so-called declaration of independence in Venezuela happened in 1797 when a group of criollos proclaimed Venezuela as an Independent Republic out of protest for the high taxes levied by the Crown against the Colonists. This failed marvelously but was a warning of things to come.

By the early years of the 1800s, the rumblings of Independence were reaching a breaking point. This was exacerbated in 1806. Here, a Venezuelan named Francisco de Miranda invaded Venezuela against the Spanish. His unique background as a General in the French Revolution and close connections with international figures like George Washington, Alexander Hamilton, and Catherine the Great gave him the pull to bring a mercenary force from the newly formed United States and a number of Caribbean nations to his home country.

Unfortunately for Miranda, the invasion did not last long. He was able to hold Coro for a few weeks but was quickly defeated by Spain and driven back out of the country. While Spain successfully resisted the physical invasion of Miranda, it had opened itself up to the invasion of independent ideas in the minds of the Venezuelan people. Miranda's invasion showed the people that independence was more than just a word, and his actions inspired many more in the years to come.

As the desire for independence in Venezuela grew, Spain was losing to France. Before long, in early 1810, Ferdinand VII became a prisoner of Napoleon in the Peninsular War and Spain's arm became too weak to properly support and focus on its Venezuelan colony. As a result, criollos patriotas in Venezuela met in Caracas on April 19, 1810. The meeting produced a provisional declaration of independence until the Spanish Crown was restored to power back in Spain.

First Venezuelan Republic

Nearly everyone agreed with this move as a form of resistance to French rule. Many planned on returning to Spanish rule as soon as the King regained power of Spain, but others saw it as only a step towards a greater victory that would be achieved over the coming years. Simón Bolívar was one of the latter. He, along with José Félix Ribas, and Francisco de Miranda, would soon establish the First Venezuelan Republic.

This government quickly outlawed slavery, exempted natives from paying tribute to the government and made some major economic changes. Not all of Venezuela followed the lead of Caracas, however. Many cities chose to remain under the weakened Spanish rule. This led to a host of infighting and a Congress of the people was called in 1811 to pursue peace.

Peace would not be achieved, but another step towards full independence would be. Many of those gathered at the Congress refused to be led by a weakened and non-effective Spanish Crown. They sent many Spanish officers back to Spain while Francisco de Miranda returned.

On July 5, 1811, the ruling junta of the First Venezuelan Republic voted for complete independence from the Spanish Crown.

Unsurprisingly, resistance was strong. A host of royalists resisted a powerful earthquake that struck Caracas on March 26, 1812, which put thorns into the side of the new government. It soon collapsed with Bolívar and Miranda sent into exile.

The Admirable Campaign

The revolutionary leaders would not abandon their country for long. In October 1912, Bolívar was given a small army by the newly liberated leaders in Colombia, called New Granada at the time. New Granada, like many of the newly forming South American nations, knew that they could not be truly independent while Spain held a foothold in the region. With this in mind, they urged Bolívar to take the force and liberate Caracas from the Spanish Crown.

Step one, however, was to remove Spain from the Magdalena River on the western side of New Granada. If successful, New Granada promised a larger force to return to Caracas in an attempt to liberate Venezuela. Bolívar started well. The force grew larger and larger as the Spaniards grew weaker and weaker. Before long, the Spaniards were gone and Bolívar returned to Cartagena, the New Grenadian capital, and gained permission to take the forces to Venezuela.

Bolívar's military success continued as he removed Spain from Caracas in August of 1813. All in all, Bolívar took one year from the end of the First Venezuelan Republic to travel to New Granada, remove Spanish influence from the Magdalena River, and return his forces back to Venezuela to remove the Spaniards. The highly successful campaign became known as the Admirable Campaign and Bolívar achieved eternal fame in Venezuelan history for the accomplishment.

The Second Venezuelan Republic

Bolívar was instrumental in establishing the next phase of Venezuelan Independence. On August 7, 1813, Bolívar declared the reestablished Venezuelan Republic after defeating Spain's Domingo Monteverde and Santiago Mariño during the Admirable Campaign.

The Infernal Legion, however, a group of Spanish loyalists led by the Spaniard Tomas Boves, did not relent. They saw the patriots' beliefs as an insult to the Spanish Crown and bluntly raided towns held by the patriots, executing prisoners and pillaging their homes. Bolívar was soon defeated once again in 1814 and was forced to return to exile for the second time.

The failure of the Venezuelan people to agree on whether or not to stay as a colony of Spain or form their own independent nation launched the region into a five-year period of war. Various patriot and royalist groups fought one another all across Venezuela. The patriots especially were quite unorganized and many groups fought independently of one another. The three most prominent leaders, Manuel Piar, José Antonio Páez and Simón Bolívar led three separate armies, none of which acknowledged the others.

Even more detrimental to the independence effort, Bolívar had Piar arrested and executed in 1817 as a notice that it was only him and his followers that were seeking the right version of independence for Venezuela. This move led most patriots to Bolívar's side as they saw him as their best chance for achieving an independent Venezuela. This collaboration, however, did not lead to a drastic change in the momentum for the patriots who still made no headway against the royalists for many years to come.

Bolívar continued to lose ground against the Spaniards until he and his army were pushed back to the western corner of the state. Here, Bolívar was forced to make a momentous decision. He had been in a stalemate with the Spaniards for weeks and had been unable to push them back. Instead of remaining in a stalemate with the Spanish, Bolívar decided to take his forces and march over the Andes in the early months of 1819.

Bolívar led his troops back to New Granada and spent the summer resting and recruiting more troops after losing nearly half over the Andes crossing. In the summer weather, the army of 3,000 strong was able to move much quicker and marched to Bogota in late June. Hearing the news of the incoming army, the Spanish hurriedly sent out a force to repel Bolívar. The patriots and Spaniards faced each other at the Battle of Boyacá on August 7, 1819 near Bogota. Bolívar's forces prevailed and marched on to capture Bogota on August 10, freeing the last Spanish-controlled city of New Granada.

After the victory at Bogota, Bolívar took his forces back into Venezuela to establish the Republic of Gran Colombia—a nation composed of present-day Venezuela, Colombia, Ecuador, and Panama. After another victory at the Battle of Carabobo, Bolívar took his troops to Caracas and pronounced the Republic in June of 1821.

República de Gran Colombia

The Congress of Cúcuta established the Republic as an independent and centralized representative republic headquartered in Bogota. Simon Bolívar was chosen as the first president with Francisco de Paula Santander, another prominent general from the independent movement, as the vice president.

The Republic was organized into three regions of government and a bicameral legislature governed with the President at the head. The merging of this wide variety of people was short lived.

Various civilian and military groups rivaled one another for power over the young nation and inequality between the three regions led to a vast amount of malcontent among the citizens. The Venezuelan region declared an open rebellion in 1826, taking the first steps to the dismantling of the new country. Bolívar fought the dissolution as President from 1821 to 1828 and as dictator from 1828 to 1830.

As a last ditch effort, Bolívar evoked a convention to create a new constitution to stabilize the regions. Colombia and Panama agreed to the new constitution but Ecuador and Venezuela refused. As a result of the failed state and subsequent failing health, Bolívar resigned and settled in the northern coast. A few weeks later he would die in an outlying town of Santa Marta on December 17, 1930, while The Republic of Gran Colombia would dissolve.

An Independent Venezuela

After the resignation of Bolívar, Venezuela, along with Ecuador, seceded from the Republic of Gran Colombia, setting the course for independent states. Like before, prominent civilian and military figures jockeyed for power and attempted to establish a functional government. This began "The Century of Caudillo" or the "Caudillismo" where the government of Venezuela would revolve around a "strong man" in a dictatorial and highly centralized government despite a democratic Constitution being ratified in 1830.

Venezuela from 1830 to 1870

This period would begin with José Antonio Páez, who was chosen as the provisional president of the newly sovereign Venezuela in 1830. His rise to power began in the Venezuelan independence movement where he had been a significant lieutenant to Bolívar for much of the independence campaign. Most significantly, he had led the patriots to victory in Carabobo in 1821 and Puerto

Cabello in 1823, the latter of which was the last significant battle with the Spanish before the groundwork of the Republic of Gran Colombia was laid.

Páez unified the country and led significant changes to the civilian and political life of the region. Most notably, he removed much of the Church's power from government affairs but still recognized Catholicism as the primary religious activity of the state and a significant religious authority. He would serve two terms—his first lasting from 1831-1835 (continuing after his 1830 year of service as the provisional president) and his second lasted from 1839-1843.

In between his terms, a host of leaders would serve in the highly unstable years of 1835-1839. These years would see the Revolution of Reforms, newly formed "liberators" of Venezuela, and disagreements over whether Páez's support of the Republic of Gran Colombia, when it had existed, was faithful to the vision Venezuelans had for their new country.

The political sphere of Venezuela would begin to stabilize in 1839 when Páez was once again chosen as the President of the nation, but economical factors would soon plunge Venezuela into yet another state of disarray.

In 1840, coffee, which had become the central export of the burgeoning nation and the base of the political and social elite's wealth, would experience a significant drop in price in the world economy. Coffee's price drop would have significant effects on the political sphere as the social criollo elite would divide into Conservative and Liberal factions. The Conservatives supported Páez's claim to leadership but Liberals desperately sought out new leadership.

From 1840 to 1870, chaos would reign as 15 Presidents—the leaders were called "President" in name but would more aptly be called dictators—would come to power over six terms. This would include a period between 1858 and 1863 known as the Federal War where Páez would claim control of the nation once again from 1861-1863 along with a host of many and varied leaders.

It would not be until 1870 when some form of stability would once again be found in Venezuela under Antonio Guzmán Blanco's leadership.

Antonio Guzmán Blanco: 1870-1889

Guzmán Blanco is still considered one of the caudillo (strongman) leaders of Venezuela, but his strength was able to unite the country and provide stability in leadership for nearly two decades. The Guzmán Blanco name was widely recognized in Venezuela prior to his leadership as a fixture of the upper class. His father, a prominent politician and journalist, had also established name recognition for the family prior to Guzmán Blanco's rise.

Guzmán Blanco was an influential provincial leader early in his career and vaulted onto the national stage when he was appointed as Special Finance Commissioner to London.

Frustrated with years of instability in the nation, however, Guzmán Blanco headed the Regeneration Movement, a group of Liberals frustrated with years of Conservative leadership and, after a brief civil war, claimed leadership over the nation in 1870. In 1872, Guzmán Blanco helped pass a new constitution that established direct election of the President and a representative government voted by all males in the nation.

In addition to the new constitution, Guzmán Blanco established a nationwide public education system, cut off state funding to the Roman Catholic Church, and furthered other Liberal ideals such as freedom of religion. This move allowed him to win the 1873 election that named him the Constitutional President of Venezuela. He continued to push Venezuela forward through a massive public works campaign. His government constructed railroads, buildings, and schools across the nation and build telegraph lines and roads around the nation with their hub in Caracas. Guzmán Blanco also pushed Venezuela into a technological revolution due to increased international trade and renewed connection between the Venezuelan states.

Beneath the surface of a growing economy and secularization, the government was far from perfect. Guzmán Blanco made no effort to support civil liberties and the press was not permitted to print anything Guzmán Blanco's government found objectionable. Guzmán Blanco also spent a significant amount of his time as President rubbing shoulders with the social elite in Europe and amassing his own fortune.

Unsurprisingly, this created extreme frustration in the Venezuelan masses. In 1877, during one of his longer trips in Europe, the people rebelled until Guzmán Blanco returned in 1878 to continue his presidency and crush the rebellion. He promptly left again for a number of years as he ruled more so from Europe than he did from Caracas.

Ultimately, Guzmán Blanco's reign would come to an end in 1889 during a coup. As a result, Guzmán Blanco would spend the remainder of his life in Paris.

Joaquín Crespo, Cipriano Castro, & Juan Vicente Gómez

For four years following the ousting of Guzmán Blanco, Venezuela underwent yet another period of political instability. A handful of groups would try and fail to re-establish a representative government until October 1892.

Joaquín Crespo

Joaquín Crespo, would seize power in yet another caudillo rebellion to name himself interim President from 1882-1894. Crespo was a loyal Liberal and had spent the majority of the last three decades fighting for Liberal leadership through the Federal War and as the Minister of War for Guzmán Blanco. He had also served as a figurehead president from 1884-1886 during one of Guzmán Blanco's many European ventures.

This time, however, Crespo's rule was his alone. After his seizure of power, he was elected constitutional president from 1894-1898. This time period would feature Venezuela's first clash with Europe since the Spanish conquistadors over half a century prior.

British Guiana, now the independent nation of Guyana, was a British Colony on the border of Venezuela. During Crespo's Presidency, a dispute arose over the placement of the border between Venezuela and British Guiana. The problem arose a few decades earlier when gold was discovered in the mostly undeveloped colony in 1877. Growing interest and colonization from the British began to chafe against the Venezuelan border and the two nations argued over the lands. Crespo's Venezuela had repeatedly sought to arbitrate the matter with Great

Britain to no avail and in 1887, Crespo broke off diplomatic ties to Great Britain until they agreed to solve the disagreement.

The problem would not be solved until many years later. In 1895, U.S. President Grover Cleveland convinced, on Venezuela's behalf, Great Britain to arbitrate the matter. In 1899, an international tribunal would address the problem but their solution would be highly in favor of Britain.

Otherwise during his presidency, Crespo created the first professional Venezuelan nation army. This would prove to be an important move during his successor's presidency to fight against a rebellion. But it would be one of these conflicts that would end Crespo's life in battle in 1898.

Cipriano Castro

A year of uncertainty would follow Crespo's leadership until once again, a strong man caudillo would take control of Venezuela.

The regime of Cipriano Castro would be marked by many firsts. He was called the Lion of the Andes after his numerous exploits as governor of his province, illegal cattle trader in Colombia, and his military background. After decades of being ruled by men of Caracas and the surrounding plains, Castro would be the first man from the mountainous region in the northwest of Venezuela to lead the country.

It would be the cattle trading that indirectly give him the ability to lead the nation. After seven years making an outrageous amount of money in Colombia, Castro was able to recruit his own private army and take advantage of the political instability caused by Crespo's death in Venezuela.

In 1899, Castro's army marched on Caracas and ousted the competition. He named himself supreme military commander of Venezuela, the first man to claim that title in Venezuela, and later was elected President.

Castro was never a popular leader in Venezuela, the bulk of his reign—which lasted from 1902 to 1908—was marked by rebellions, assassinations, and unstable foreign policy. Nearly all of it stemmed from his own corruption. Castro made himself and his cronies extremely rich through their authoritarian regime and taking advantage of foreign diplomats.

His disregard for foreign entities would lead to serious problems for himself and his nation, especially in 1902 when a coalition of British, German, and Italian ships set up a blockade of Venezuelan ports to force Castro to pay his debts. While Venezuela had encountered disagreements with Europe states before—such as the border disagreement with Great Britain's colony—this would be the first time Europe would send troops to intervene with Venezuela since the removal of Spanish power from the region. The blockade would be accompanied by internal rebellion as well as Venezuelans voiced their discontent with their President.

Despite the unrest, Castro remained president until 1908 where two factors forced him to abdicate the highest office in Venezuela. After years of excess, Castro's health began to fail and he was forced to seek medical attention in Europe; at the same time, the Dutch attacked the Venezuelan navy due to financial disagreements with Castro and his regime.

Juan Vicente Gómez

When Castro left for Europe, Juan Vicente Gómez would be the next man to seize power. Gómez had nearly no formal education, but he had served as an officer to Cipriano Castro in his coup army in 1899. Castro enjoyed his support so much that he named Gómez Vice President in 1899 when Castro seized Caracas.

Gómez had supported Castro loyally throughout his term as Vice President. After all, he was the general responsible for putting down the internal revolt in 1902-1903 while Castro dealt with the foreign blockaders. As the Vice President to Castro, Gómez was the next in line to rule the unruly Venezuelan state when Castro left for Europe in 1908. Despite many who opposed him, Gómez would make significant progress towards economic stability and independence during his regime

Unfortunately for many, Gómez proved to be even more corrupt and ruthless than his predecessor. He outright manipulated elections to ensure the permanence of his power and raised hell for anyone who opposed him. To do this, Gómez banned political activity and created a legislature and judicial system loyal only to him. Like many of his predecessors, he also banned the press from publishing stories disagreeable to him and had a long line of imprisonments and assassinations that occurred to his opponents during the time.

Gómez accomplished this through the formation and organization of the strongest police and army force seen yet in Venezuela. Furthermore, he funded it through contracts with foreign petroleum companies, especially after the discovery of oil in 1914 near Lake Maracaibo. The regime struck agreements with The United States, Great Britain and the Netherlands to allow foreign companies into the region. Not only did this establish a positive international presence for Venezuela, it also absolved the many debts Castro had occurred for Venezuela prior to Gómez's leadership.

During World War I, Venezuela's economy skyrocketed as the world needed more oil than ever before. Venezuela would soon become the world's largest exporter of oil in 1928 under Gómez's rule. The staggering profits from Venezuelan's newly found oil business would drastically change the country's place on the world scale. The profits, however, had little effect on the everyday Venezuelan. Although a public works program improved the infrastructure in the nation, most of the profits landed in the pockets of the social and political elite, including Gómez himself who became considered the wealthiest man in all of South America.

The public works campaign would improve roads, railroads, and ports, but this mostly served to make even more money for Venezuela's elite. Meanwhile, most of the citizens were in working class jobs and lacked proper healthcare, housing or education.

That enormous influx of money, however, would give Gómez the power to rule for the longest period yet by a Venezuelan. From 1908 to 1935, Gómez held onto his presidential power until he died of natural causes.

Gómez's rule would permanently change Venezuela. What once was a background country hardly relevant on the world scene was now in control of the most demanded resource in the world. The oil in Venezuela would fuel the world, and Venezuela's own economic progression for the next several decades to come. Venezuela was now one of the richest nations in Latin America and held a bargaining tool the whole world desired.

Venezuela From 1935 to1958

After 27 years under Gómez, Venezuela had achieved the most economic progress and political stability seen yet in the South American nation. After Gómez, his war minister <u>Eleazar López Medina</u> would succeed him and hold the presidency for six years until 1941.

Medina lifted the iron first of Gómez slightly as he allowed citizens to reclaim civil liberties including the right to organize for political purposes. This lasted only a year, however, as he restored his dictatorship in 1937 when opposition groups threatened to remove him from power.

Medina then focused on building more public buildings such as schools and hospitals.

He would soon be succeeded by Isaias Medina Angarita, a former military general, who would restore liberties once again. 1941 would see widespread panic in Venezuela, however, as World War II caused a cut in transportation capabilities, therefore reducing Venezuela's capabilities to make money off of their oil. This would end after a year, but as a result, Medina passed a 1943 law to give the government a share of all oil profits from Venezuelan exports.

An oil boom occurred shortly thereafter and the government and political elite made fortunes off of the renewed worldwide need for the resource. Despite the massive rise in profits, Medina was overthrown in October 1945 by the Democratic Action political party—made up of a group of political leaders and military officers.

Democratic Action Leadership

A junta was formed of civilian and military leaders with Rómulo Betancourt at the head. He would rule for 28 months until a new constitution was enacted in July 1947, but would not be gone from the national stage. The new constitution featured the first appearance of leftist philosophy in the country. Soon after, Rómulo Gallegos was elected President and a host of leftist reforms began.

Most prominently, the oil industry in Venezuela was severely affected by a new tax that gave the government half of all petroleum profits. These funds were largely used to spur on reforms in labor, education, and healthcare throughout the nation.

The drastic changes were heavily opposed by Conservative leaders—the group that had largely been in power since Venezuela's independence in 1830. As a result, Conservative leaders staged a coup with the military in November 1948 and removed the leftists from power.

Back to Dictatorship, For Now

For the first time in its history, Venezuela now had two leaders—a phenomenon all too familiar to present day Venezuelan citizens. This time, however, the leaders worked together as Major Marcos Pérez Jiménez and Lieutenant Colonel Carlos Delgado Chalbaud headed up a new junta. The dual leadership was brief at best though as Delgado Chalbaud was assassinated two years later leaving Pérez Jiménez with sole control of the nation. In addition to the two years sharing duties with Delgado Chalbaud, Pérez Jiménez ruled from 1951 to 1958 as a military dictator in the style of many past Venezuelan leaders.

Pérez Jiménez once again banned any political or labor organizing and shutdown the press. He also shut down universities that had been newly formed in the brief Democratic Action junta. Power was removed from the Democratic Action's reforms and were placed back into the hands of the dictator and the central government of Caracas.

After the brief Democratic Action leadership, however, people found many flaws in the dictatorial system and opposition—most notably composed of army and air force troops—combined to overthrow in January of 1958. Once again, a civilian-military junta led the country for a short time until Rómulo Betancourt was again elected President.

Rómulo Betancourt

Betancourt had a long history of political activity well before his leadership in 1945. He started as a protester while studying at the University of Caracas in 1928. He actively spoke out against then leader, Juan Vincente Gómez and even after being released from jail, participated in demonstrations against the leader. This would lead to his first exile, from 1928-1936 when Gómez's government booted him out for his political activities. Betancourt would spend those eight years largely in Costa Rica writing a book about his experiences and political leanings.

In 1936, he would return again to Venezuela after Gómez was replaced by Medina, but was soon exiled again in 1939.Betancourt was able to make some reforms during his first stint as provisional President before he was succeeded by Gallegos, who continued many of his policies. Quite humorously, Betancourt was exiled for a third time when Gallegos was removed from power by Pérez Jiménez's government.

The next 10 years would see Betancourt in various North American nations until he returned to Venezuela after Pérez Jiménez's removal from power.

His many years of faithfulness to democratic ideals in Venezuela were rewarded when Betancourt was elected democratically in 1959. He inherited a split country bent between communists sympathizing with the rising regime of Fidel Castro in Cuba and Conservatives seeking a return to the strong dictatorial ideals of Venezuela's past.

Betancourt successfully found the middle ground for the next several years, finding support from the Christian Democrats, otherwise known as the Social Christian Party. Betancourt was able to form a coalition government between the Democratic Action Party he had founded and the Christian Democrats. In a wave of rising political tension throughout South America and the world—most notably the growing Cold War between The United States and Soviet Union, which started in 1946 and was soon to grow in to a fever pitch with the Cuban Missile Crisis in 1962.

Despite this tension, Betancourt was able to guide the country to modernization in agriculture—now the second most important economic activity in Venezuela behind oil—healthcare and education. This was the first time in Venezuela's history where illiteracy was all but eliminated throughout the country. This helped create a host of industrial development that allowed Venezuela to add variance to its economy.

Betancourt's most notable contributions to Venezuelan legislature occurred with his agrarian reform law in 1960 and his inauguration of a nationalized steel industry in 1962. Betancourt would leave office in 1964 and exile himself to Switzerland for the next eight years.

Near the end of Betancourt's leadership an insurgency of guerilla fighters had formed in the nation claiming that Betancourt had abandoned the ideals for which he was elected. This claim was supported by an economic depression in 1960 and 1963 and Venezuela's tumultuous international relations as a founding member of OPEC along with conflict with the Dominican Republic and Cuba.

The Cold War in Venezuela

Leoni & Modernization

In 1963, Betancourt was replaced by Raúl Leoni, a fellow member of the Democratic Action party and another one of its founding members. Instead of the Christian Democrats, however, his coalition government would be formed with the Democratic Republic Union, a pro-labor, leftist party growing in popularity within the nation.

Like his predecessor, Leoni had been politically active since he was a youth and had also organized against Gómez in 1928, resulting in his own exile for eight years. After a few more issues with the rotation of leaders Venezuela experienced in the early to mid 1900s, Leoni earned a law degree in Colombia and returned to the side of Betancourt. He served as a Minister of Labor during Betancourt's presidency, overseeing collective bargaining agreements in the oil industry, and also gained experience with the International Labor Organization with the United Nations.

Leoni's presidency lasted from 1964 to 1968 and was mostly a continuation of Betancourt's work. Leoni continued to focus on improving industrialization within the country while expanding education throughout the nation. Notably, Leoni was the first leader to recognize the Communist Party as a legal entity, which he did near the end of his term in 1968. During the presidency, oil and iron continued to grow in value throughout the world and Venezuela focused on making both principal exports. Leoni oversaw the new petrochemical industry as well, leading to increased exports. Furthermore, Leoni would start a trend that would continue for many years to come as he took a note out of former leaders' books by increasing taxation on oil companies.

The First Presidency of <u>*Rafael Caldera Rodríguez*</u>

Leoni was replaced in the 1968 election by Rafael Caldera Rodríguez, the first Christian Democrat elected to the highest office of Venezuela. Holding a doctorate in political science from the Central University of Venezuela, Caldera Rodríguez had begun his political life as a member of Congress in 1941 and followed it up with four unsuccessful candidacies for president.

In 1968, however, he would prevail and for the first time in Venezuelan history, the incumbent government peacefully transitioned power to the newly elected junta. Caldera Rodríguez instituted a marked change to foreign policy as he quickly worked to form better relationships with Cuba, the Soviet Union, and the various military dictatorships throughout South America, most notably Argentina, Panama, and Peru.

He allowed leftist political activists to return to the country, granting them amnesty and encouraging peaceful discourse on politics. Like many of his predecessors, Caldera Rodríguez also focused on investing thought and resources into non-oil industries to diversify Venezuela's export and prevent problems, should the price of oil drop. The most notable in these were Venezuela's investment into many foreign banks, giving them majority ownership.

The First Presidency of <u>*Carlos Andrés Pérez*</u>

After Caldera Rodríguez, the Christian Democrat party was replaced by the Democratic Action party. This time, Carlos Andrés Pérez, a longtime member of the party since its founding by Betancourt, was elected to the presidency in 1974.

Betancourt would return to Venezuela for the first time in eight years after his self-imposed exile to Switzerland to support Andrés Pérez for the presidency. This support gave Andrés Pérez an easy victory and allowed him to handle Venezuela's biggest problem—managing the ever-growing petroleum industry—for the next several years.

The industry's tremendous success led to a wave of foreign investment, especially since Betancourt's leadership had established more political stability to the region.

The government of Andrés Pérez and the Venezuelan oil industry also received unexpected help from elsewhere in the world. The Arab-Israeli War of 1973 led to a significant reduction in oil production among many of Venezuela's most significant competitors. This allowed OPEC, of which Venezuela was a principal member, to triple the price of oil and bring waves of new profits into the nation. Now, Andrés Pérez had to navigate a host of foreign control on Venezuela's oil fields and choose how to invest the massive government profits from the industry.

Andrés Pérez chose to invest in small businesses and agriculture, widening the effect of petroleum profits beyond the social and political elite whom the profits had served most notably over the last several decades. He also invested money in steel mills and hydroelectric power—Venezuela's geography is home to a host of rivers—and followed his predecessors by continuing to invest heavily in public education. The growing wave in government spending led to a significant increase in immigration from Venezuela's South American neighbors. While this increased diversity and strengthened the economy of Venezuela, it also led to growing corruption in a stronger economic elite. The significant wealth gap that had been present in Venezuela since the discovery of oil became even more apparent during this time.

Venezuela under Andrés Pérez also established the most peaceful and successful foreign policy to date. Andrés Pérez was able to successfully navigate the world tension still present from the Cold War through improving Venezuelan's relationships with the United States, fresh off the Watergate conspiracy and under the leadership of President Gerald R. Ford.

At the same time, Andrés Pérez re-established Venezuela's relationship with Cuba, which had been broken off by Betancourt. This may have been one of the primary reasons why Betancourt broke his relationship with Andrés Pérez late in Andrés Pérez's presidency. Andrés Pérez also gained an ally in Panama as he, while maintaining friendship with the United States, supported their claim to control the Panama Canal.

Andrés Pérez's term would end in 1979, which would be just in time to save his popularity. Despite the economic recession that occurred after his term—largely a result of an international recession and the slashing of oil prices—Andrés Pérez maintained a spectacular reputation amongst his people. The popularity would be strong enough to return him back to the center of Venezuelan politics soon.

Luis Herrera Campíns

Following the first term of Andrés Pérez, Luis Herrera Campíns was elected president in 1979.

Internationally, the Cold War was still raging. A Strategic Arms Limitation Agreement had fallen through between U.S. President Jimmy Carter and Soviet Union leader Leonid Brezhnev after the Soviets invaded Afghanistan.

Elsewhere Ayatollah Ruhollah Khomeini returned to Tehran, Iran, removed the Shah of Persia, and changed the Iranian government—one of the world's largest oil producers—to an Islamic Republic.

Herrera Campíns came to the presidency, like many before him, with a wide range of political backgrounds. Like most of his predecessors, he had been exiled from the nation in protest to former Venezuelan dictators and had helped the Christian Democrats become the second largest party in Venezuela.

Unfortunately for him, unlike his predecessors, Herrera Campíns came to power at the beginning of an economic downturn. He was further hamstrung by his Congress, where his party did not have a majority and he struggled to pass legislation. Herrera Campíns was able to devalue Venezuela's currency for the first time in two decades, but that measure proved ineffective to help Venezuelan's crashing economy.

Unsurprisingly, Herrera Campíns and the Christian Democrat party were not reelected in 1983.

Jaime Ramón Lusinchi

Next up to lead Venezuela would be Democratic Action party member Lusinchi, elected to the presidency in 1983. Like Herrera Campíns, he would be thrust into a country in the midst of an economic downturn. Lusinchi would also be hampered by a social scandal with his secretary, Blanca Ibáñez, who became increasingly prominent in his government, as the two engaged in sexual activity with one another.

The challenge to his reputation along with poor economic conditions led to poor popularity for Lusinchi. He was able to pass austerity policies to help control the country's debt at first, but made an interesting later move in his presidency to increase spending, likely to improve his reputation. The move worked and his public support increased near the end of his presidency, but inflation only became worse.

In all fairness, it was not only Venezuela suffering from significant economic decline during this time period. 1988 saw a drastic decrease in oil prices and other countries in economic downturn became increasingly in need of payments on Venezuelan debt.

The presidency that was marked by scandal would end in scandal as well; Lusinchi soon faced allegations of fraud forcing him to flee the country with Ibáñez until 1997 when the charges were dropped after exceeding their statute of limitations.

Stalemate

The next several years would include a host of familiar faces on the Venezuelan political scene. Little progress would be made and the Venezuelan people would soon become extremely frustrated with the political stalemate created by the two-party system (Democratic Action vs. Christian Democrats). These next few years would set the stage for a political revolution that would have an effect that would ripple far beyond the borders of Venezuela, and even South America.

The Second Presidency of Carlos Andrés Pérez

It had been previously established—likely as a result of the carousel of dictators experienced by the country in the 19th century—by the Venezuelan constitution that any president would be barred by law from seeking re-election for 10 years following their term.

In 1989, those 10 years were up for Andrés Pérez. Considering his significant popularity coming out of his first presidency, it was no surprise that, after deciding to seek re-election, the Venezuelan people once again turned to him. This would be the first time in a quarter of a century that any political party in Venezuela would maintain leadership of the nation.

While the international community was recovering from the end of the Cold War—marked by the removal of the Berlin Wall, the deposition of Soviet leaders throughout the bulk of Europe, the death of Japanese emperor Hirohito, and unrest in China—a growing world power—with protests in Tiananmen Square. Growing peace amongst the international community, however, would see increased oil production in the Middle East and a slowdown in demand for oil across the world. Venezuelans saw Andrés Pérez as their best hope for returning to the period of growth they had last experienced under his leadership.

It was soon discovered, however, that Andrés Pérez was not the savior of the economy Venezuelans were looking for. The economy continued to decline and, after a package of austerity measures released by Andrés Pérez upon election in early 1989, riots began to ensue. One of the biggest complaints was an increased bus fair instituted as a part of those austerity measures that took its toll on a poor population who largely took the bus to work each day.

Riots ensued for the bulk of the first year of his term marked by looting and hundreds of citizens killed in the military's attempt to quell the discontent. Even after the end of the riots, Andrés Pérez's government was troubled by labor strikes and massive political frustrations with his foreign policy and handling of the economy.

Furthermore, two separate coups attempted to remove him from office in 1992, the first of which led by quite possibly the most famous name in Venezuelan politics today, Hugo Chávez. The coup would fail and Chávez was imprisoned.

A few months later, officers in the Air Force attempted to remove him as well. Both coup attempts failed, but legal troubles did not and Andrés Pérez was arrested for misusing public funds and embezzling money from the government. He was removed from office in 1993. Other than a brief stint as a senator from 1996 to 1998, this would mark the end of his political life in Venezuela.

The Second Presidency _Rafael Caldera_

With Andrés Pérez removed from office, Venezuela experienced another brief period of political instability. Two interims served until elections could be held in late 1993 for the 1994 term. Again, a former President was chosen as Rafael Caldera returned to office.

This time, however, Caldera did not run for President with the Christian Democratic Party that he had founded and successfully procured election with during his first term. For his second term, in 1994, when he ran for the presidency for the sixth time, he was supported by a large group of smaller leftist parties, but he was still largely seen as a member of the establishment and a facilitator of the corruption which had continued to plague the Venezuelan government for a number of years.

Caldera attempted to solve the continued corruption perceived by the Venezuelan people in the executive branch. He went so far as to create a "Presidential Commission to Combat Corruption" and make corruption a major theme—much to the frustration of other foreign leaders more interested in economic integration—in the Venezuelan-hosted Ibero-American Summit in 1997.

Despite his outspoken efforts of corruption, many critics argue his policies demonstrate the exact opposite. Controls on pricing and foreign exchanges were claimed to increase the possibility for corruption and his failure to bring justice to bankers in the financial industry both led to pointed attacks that he provided an environment for corruption and hurt the struggling economy even further.

Caldera also spoke outwardly against capitalism. Especially during the end of this term, Caldera shifted significant control of the banks, foreign exchange agencies to the government and interfered with many constitutional rights. This would lay the groundwork for the political scene in Venezuela for decades to come.

Venezuela Under Hugo Chávez

During the 1998 elections, Venezuela had experienced the worst run of their economy yet. Half of the populace was below the poverty line, oil prices continued to drop, and the policies of the Christian Democrats and Democratic Action parties had failed to satisfy Venezuelans' growing needs.

Despite his rebellious actions during the coup, Chávez represented an attractive alternative. Unlike his predecessors, Chávez had never before held political office and had spent the previous two decades serving in the military. He was a devout follower of the ideologies of Simon Bolívar—Venezuela's Founding Father—and Karl Marx.

He spoke of a Bolivarian Revolution based upon the socialist politics he read from Karl Marx. He preached a strong military, centralized economy and firm faith in Venezuela. His politics would soon simply be called "chavismo" and represent much of who he was as a young man, a passionate Venezuelan who chafed against rules and establishment.

He spoke out against corruption that he saw as a major problem for the country's working class, and committed himself to help the many poor people in the country. Chávez's speeches energized a Venezuelan populous that had spent the last decade in the worst economy of their lifetime.

President Chávez

In 1998, Hugo Chávez was elected as President under these pledges as well as a promise to rewrite the Venezuelan constitution. By 1999, most of the legislature was made up of Chávez supporters and a referendum passed the constitution Chávez had promised.

Unfortunately, the following year would see tragedy for millions of Venezuelans. A severe rainstorm in December 1999 along the northern mountains and coast caused significant damage throughout the country. It is estimated that hundreds of thousands were killed in the flash floods, mud slides, and destroyed structures throughout the nation. This would turn out to be one of the deadliest natural events in South American history. For the rest of his term, Chávez would have to keep the reconstruction of this region of Venezuela as one of his top priorities in order to develop the nation.

Through Chávez's reconstruction projects and his leftist policies, the working class supported him and applauded his programs to provide education, food, and social services to even the poorest of Venezuelans. Other Venezuelans saw the reforms as unfair, however, and were worried about Chávez's close ties with Fidel Castro in Cuba. This caused 2001, the third year of his term, to be marked by protests and strikes throughout the country. Chávez largely ignored the protests and continued to pass policies supporting his agenda while limiting free speech throughout the country.

Chávez would also break the ties that former Venezuelan leaders had worked to establish with the Western power, the United States. Chávez developed close foreign ties to countries in the Middle East, especially Iraq and Iran, two of the biggest enemies to the United States. He also criticized the United States when the September 11 attacks on New York City prompted an invasion of Iraq.

None of these moves were particularly popular amongst Venezuelans and his approval rating dropped significantly. This unrest would be followed by a 2002 rally in Venezuela on April 11 with an estimated million people marching in protest of Chávez. Chávez called in the Venezuelan National Guard, which responded by shooting into the civilian masses. The civilians shot back and a host of casualties occurred on both sides. This caused the military to revolt and take Chávez into custody.

Despite the widespread disagreements with Chávez, the move was labeled a coup and the military's interim government, led by the businessman Pedro Carmona, was quickly removed after Carmona dissolved many of Venezuela's democratic processes in his first day in charge.

Two days later, Chávez would again be sworn in as President on April 14, 2002. These disagreements amongst the Venezuelans continued through a general strike in 2002 seeking early elections and Chávez's resignation. This was especially potent when PDVSA, one of the largest Venezuelan companies and responsible for a large majority of Venezuela's exports, went on strike.

Chávez did not relent. Instead of hearing out the workers' claims and resigning, he fired every striking worker and hired additional people willing to work. By early 2003, PDVSA was back to full production, the strike was made ineffective, and Chávez now had significant control over Venezuela's petroleum business.

Despite the setback in the PDVSA strike, the opposition to Chávez did not back off either. 2003 and 2004 saw opposition politicians seek a referendum to remove Chávez from office. Chávez, on the other hand, cleverly used his profits from PDVSA to invest in education and health care initiatives, skyrocketing his approval ratings. The referendum gained enough support to go to a vote, but by that time, Chávez's approval allowed him to receive three-fifths of the vote.

Chávez also used his power to reduce the influence of the United States in Latin America. For this task, his primary tool was oil. He offered his oil at lower prices to developing nations, most notably, Cuba, and used Venezuela's profits and economic influence in the region to add strength to Mercado Común Del Sur—meaning Common Market of the South in English but most easily recognized by the name Mercosur—an economic organization focused on growing the regional economies in South America.

His initially unpopular policies were able to gain enough support that in 2006, Chávez was re-elected, this time to a six-year term as president in a 63% victory. This victory was accompanied with some question marks, however, as allegations of fraud surrounded him, especially with his overwhelming support from members of the National Election Council. This caused the opposition to boycott legislative election, a move that may have benefited Chávez supporters even further as they gained full control over the National Assembly.

Chávez continued to lead Venezuela through his socialist agenda, nationalizing the oil, electric, and telecommunications industry. For this first time, the government now had complete control over the oil industry, which included the largest oil repository in the world—the Orinoco basin. Chávez also continued fighting against United States power throughout the region. He called President W. Bush "the Devil" during a visit to the U.N. General Assembly, he instituted Venezuela's own time zone by pushing the clocks back a half hour back, and continued to provide cut-rate oil to many Latin American nations to reduce their reliance on the United States.

In the meantime, Chávez continued growing popular support amongst Venezuelans through a variety of measures. This included capping the work day at six hours and increasing financial support to the healthcare industry and educational infrastructure.

President for Life

The support, while significantly greater than he had experienced during the early years of the 2000s, was not quite what he wished. Near the end of 2007, Chávez proposed a constitutional referendum that would have given him the ability to run for indefinite reelection, overturning the provision that an elected President may not run again for a period of ten years (If you recall, this was the provision that caused the 10-year separation between Betancourt's two terms in the mid-1900s).

The referendum would become Chávez's first loss among the people. The change was voted down 51 to 49 percent, barely preventing Chávez from being able to run for President indefinitely. This proved to be a minor speed bump at best, however, as Chávez continued to pass his leftist agenda throughout the late 2000s, which included a constitutional change with different wording that allowed Chávez to achieve his goal of indefinitely reelection anyway with a 54 percent majority.

This would be followed by aggressive anti-opposition movements throughout the Chávez government. Political opponents were arrested at higher numbers and the little press that remained critical of the Chávez regime were shut down by agents of the Venezuelan government.

Venezuela's brand on the international scene would continue to change. In addition to continued alienation of the United States by the Chávez administration, tension with their longtime ally, Colombia, would also occur.

A group of <u>leftwing revolutionaries</u>, the Fuerzas Armadas Revolucionarias de Colombia (FARC) and the Ejército de Liberación Nacional (ELN) had formed in Colombia in the early 1960s as Betancourt grew in popularity within Venezuela. Both the FARC and ELN were inspired by Cuba's Fidel Castro and promoted similar ideologies to Chávez. They had also both been condemned by the United States as foreign terrorists.

By 2002, Álvaro Uribe had been elected President of Colombia and had fought hard against the rebel groups. This pushed many FARC and ELN members out of the country and allegedly, many went to Venezuela where they hoped Chávez would be sympathetic to their ideologies. This caused the Colombian government to accuse Chávez of sheltering the rebels in July 2010, leading Chávez to break off diplomatic ties with Colombia for a time until a conciliatory meeting occurred a month later between Chávez and the recently elected Colombian President <u>Juan Manuel Santos</u> who would go on to win a Nobel Peace Prize in 2016.

The Beginning of the End

Soon after, the Chávez administration experienced a scare as the President was flown out to Cuba for a cancer operation in June 2011. Speculations about his health went flying across the lips of Venezuelan people and the international community, especially when Chávez returned to Cuba for follow-up visits and treatment. His political life remained unchanged, though, as he aggressively campaigned for re-election in 2012 against Henrique Capriles Radonski, possibly the strongest opponent Chávez had faced since his first election in 1998. Capriles Radonski had managed to unite 30 different opposition parties against Chávez and mount what started as a promising campaign to win the election.

Chávez still managed to win the election by over 10 percent in October 2012 before flying to Cuba for additional cancer treatment afterwards. It was before this trip that Chávez first announced a successor. In a move that is still having profound implications across the Venezuelan political landscape—mostly because there was no provision in the constitution or elsewhere for a successor to be chosen by Chávez—Nicolás Maduro was named the successor to the Venezuelan presidency.

Chávez survived the late 2012 surgery in Cuba, but spent many weeks in Cuba recovering from what many said was a lung infection that occurred after the surgery. Similar to his first trip to Cuba, however, details were not released by the government and the people knew very little about their President's health. Nevertheless, this gave Maduro a taste of the highest office in Venezuela as Chávez's health continued to fail.

This issue became more potent in January 2013 when Chávez was unable to return to Venezuela for his inauguration. A constitutional issue arose in which many in the opposition began calling for the head of the National Assembly to become the interim president while Chávez recovered. The Supreme Court disagreed and permitted the inauguration to be delayed. Their decision proved to be about meaningless on March 5, 2013 when

Hugo Chávez died at the age of 58 leaving Maduro as the interim President of Venezuela.

A special election occurred a few weeks later on April 14, 2013 in which Madura was confirmed as the next President of Venezuela to finish Chávez's six year term.

Nicolás Maduro and Venezuela Today

The death of Chávez, though welcome to many who chafed against his policies, caused Venezuela to be one of the most politically unstable countries since his death. Maduro, as the chosen successor from Chávez, won a small victory over his opponent Capriles among a host of allegations of election fraud.

Maduro, like many of Venezuela's early dictators grew up in Caracas for most of his life. His father had been a supporter of Fidel Castro in Cuba and Maduro had gotten involved in politics early foregoing a university education to train as a political organizer in Cuba. He came back to Venezuela to work as a cab driver and lead a political union of transit workers. At the same time, he became an avid supporter of Chávez and argued for his release after Chávez's 1994 imprisonment.

In 1999, during the early years of Chávez's presidency, Maduro was a member of the National Constituent Assembly and partook in the rewriting of Venezuela's constitution, an essential part of Chávez's early presidency. After the constitution was passed, Maduro was elected into the lower Venezuelan legislature—The Chamber of Deputies—until Venezuela shifted to a unicameral National Assembly. Maduro would be elected to this as well in 2005 and would be named the President of the National Assembly in 2006. This gave him a platform for international relations as a foreign minister.

It was only in Chávez's last campaign for presidency that Maduro became the Vice President. It didn't hurt Maduro that his wife, who had long been an influential attorney in Venezuela well before their wedding, was named Attorney General at the same time. When Chávez left for Cuba, Maduro locked in his future when he was named as the successor to Chávez should he fail to return to the Presidency.

President Maduro

As Maduro gained power, the Venezuelan economy began to slow. A host of basic materials such as toiletries, milk, and flour became expensive and rare across the country and many became frustrated with Maduro's failure to solve the problem. Crime rates grew, and the government was soon forced to intervene to protests from an extremely frustrated middle class in Caracas and San Crisóbal in February of 2014. The working class, on the other hand, tended to be big supporters of Maduro. This included a large portion of military and police members who would serve to secure Maduro's presidency for years to come.

The reduction of oil prices around the world continued to harm the Venezuelan economy, as did a shift in oil production. Crude oil in Venezuela was becoming more prominently vicious petroleum, which increased the overhead necessary for Venezuela to refine the oil and export it. A financial ecosystem that had been built around their petroleum sales for the last several decades saw clearly their failure to diversify the economy. GDP plummeted and inflation increased as jobs became increasingly difficult to find and the companies that had fueled the Venezuelan economy, both with their oil and their revenues, struggled to make a profit.

Maduro recognized the issue but shifted the focus of his brand to foreign affairs. He relied heavily on Venezuela's alliance with Fidel Castro in Cuba to survive and attempted to shift Venezuelans focus from the internal struggles to a border dispute with Guyana that had fallen mostly to the background since the arbitration with Britain when the land had been a colony under their empire. This became an even bigger focus of Maduro when oil was found in May of 2015 along the disputed shoreline.

Struggles occurred on Venezuela's western border as well when three Venezuelan military officers were shot near the border of Colombia in August of 2015. This, along with a growing concern of Colombian smugglers caused

Maduro to deport over a thousand Colombians as tens of thousands followed in their own self-imposed Diaspora fearing retribution from Maduro.

Despite Maduro's emphasis on foreign affairs, Venezuelans remained largely concerned with their inability to acquire basic goods. On December 6, 2015, a legislative election showed that the people had lost significant confidence in Maduro by giving a new centrist-conservative opposition a significant majority in the legislature.

A gridlock would occur over the next several months as the new conservative majority would free many political opponents Maduro had jailed during the early part of his campaign and Maduro would continue to defend the social reforms passed by both his and Chávez's governments.

A Country in Crisis

Maduro's troubles as President of Venezuela were only beginning. In April 2016, power became a massive issue throughout the country as the grid—fueled in large amount by a hydroelectric system set up decades earlier—ran low on power in the severe drought. The government cut the work week to two days and protests and riots began to run rampant across the nation.

Political woes continued as well as 1.8 million Venezuelans signed a petition to vote on removing Maduro from the presidency. Corruption would once again interfere, however, as the Election Commission made up primarily of Maduro supporters slowed the process. It would finally move through in May 2016 but would be faced with claims from Maduro that the signatures were falsified. This political move allowed the recall to be delayed and change the potential outcome of the recall. By slowing it and making the recall unable to occur in 2016, Maduro ensured that even a successful recall would not result in a special election, but instead in the elevation of his Vice President to the office.

The Electoral Commission denied Maduro's claims of forged signature in August, but did not set a date for the second step in procuring a recall vote, leading to widespread protests on September 1, 2016 throughout the country under the banner "Takeover of Caracas." Dates were set soon after, placating the demonstrators briefly until lower courts claimed fraud.

The opposition also passed legislation to reduce presidential terms back to four years instead of the six that the constitution had been changed to allow during the Chávez years. The motion passed, but the Supreme Court ruled that the change could not be introduced retroactively, meaning, Maduro's term would be unaffected.

This only proved to worsen the situation as demonstrations and violence increased throughout the country. Maduro responded by declaring a State of Emergency in Venezuela on May 13, 2016, claiming that foreign powers and right wing extremists were colluding to create anarchy in the state. Military and police forces were called in to maintain order despite a rejection from the National Assembly.

Venezuelans, meanwhile, were in squalor. This was demonstrated most potently when an estimated 100,000 Venezuelans took advantage of a rare and brief opening of the Colombian border in July 2016 to cross the border and buy basic items like food, toiletries, and medicine. This caught the attention of the United Nations and Ban Ki-Moon, Secretary-General of the U.N. announced that Venezuela was experiencing a "humanitarian crisis" as a result of their economic and political instability. Even the Pope, Francis I—incidentally the first pope from Latin America—would speak to Maduro and urge the nation to take action on behalf of its struggling people.

Representatives from the Maduro government were quick to deny the claim from the U.N and continued to reduce the international community's vantage point on their struggling country.

No Solution in Sight

Maduro responded by increasing his arrests of the political opposition and refused any humanitarian aid from foreign countries. Many political pundits believe that this was a refusal to admit that Venezuela was indeed in a crisis despite a 19% drop in GDP and 800% inflation rate according to the central bank (this information, note well, was a leak, the central bank had stopped releasing information well before this, presumably on instruction from the Maduro administration).

Even the opposition majority in the National Assembly was unable to institute changes. After nearly 20 years of PSUV power (the party of Chávez and Maduro) the Supreme Court was made up almost exclusively of Maduro supporters and struck down every legislation passed by Maduro's opponents in The National Assembly. The Supreme Court went so far as to dissolve the legislature in March 2017 and declaring the group in contempt of court due to charges of election fraud.

This perceived power grab was picked up immediately by the rest of the world and widespread condemnation from various world leaders forced Maduro to overturn the move and reinstate the legislature.

Overturning the move had little to no effect on the morale of the Venezuelan people. Protests lined the streets for weeks and became even worse when Capriles, the politician who had run against Maduro in the 2014 presidential election, was banned from running for public office for a period of 15 years. Violence ensued as conflicts popped up in Caracas and across the country. By June, it was approximated that more than a thousand people had been injured and about 60 people were killed.

June also saw an attack on the Supreme Court. Protestors appeared in what was claimed to be a stolen police helicopter above the Supreme Court on June 27. Gunfire and grenades pelted the building, prompting Maduro to label the move a "terrorist attack" and condemn his opposition.

The Venezuelan people continued to revolt under Maduro's reign as the state of affairs in Venezuela remained corrupt and volatile.

Finally the time for election came in July 30, 2017. Concerned about the fairness of the election after numerous power grabs from Maduro, the opposition chose to boycott the election and protest instead. In the confusion, a number of opposition leaders were killed and this prompted the United States to freeze all of Maduro's assets and block trade with Venezuela in addition to sanctions against him and many of his associates.

The next several months would see even more controversy over elections and an absolutely destroyed Venezuelan economy. Not only was the country suffering from a lack of production and exports, they were also faced with massive sanctions from all around the world. The Bolivar, the country's currency, is all but worthless and even a shift to the *petro*, a cryptocurrency introduced by Maduro, could not rectify Venezuela's economic woes.

An early election was called in May 2018 and, with most of the notable opposition jailed, Maduro procured control of the country until 2025 through his version of legality. Unsurprisingly, the opposition cried out heavily in protest with allegations of fraudulent results backed by the United States, Canada, and a host of other Latin American countries.

Disagreements escalated even further when an assassination attempt occurred on Maduro on August 4, 2018 with drones.

Venezuela Today

On January 23, 2019, the head of the National Assembly and elected leader of the opposition, Juan Guiadó, claimed the election of Maduro was fraudulent and named himself acting President of Venezuela. A host of countries, including many of the same that critiqued the 2018 elections, rushed to recognize Guiadó as the legitimate leader. They were not unanimous though, as Russia claimed Guiadó represented a United States conspiracy and announced they would maintain their support of Maduro.

Guiadó proceeded by traveling to Colombia, breaking a travel ban instituted on Venezuelans by Maduro, and attempted to bring stockpiled international aid back into Venezuela. Violence ensured as Maduro's security forces attacked demonstrators protecting the aid trucks with tear gas and non-lethal bullets. This would repeat itself again when demonstrators attempted the same thing on the Brazilian border.

Despite Guiadó's actions, the military has remained a strong supporter of Maduro and has thus far prevented anyone from usurping him.

Now, according to the BBC, Venezuela is still in a state of disarray with little hope of rectification. Four million Venezuelans have left the country—mostly to Colombia, Peru, The United States, Ecuador, and Spain—and those that remain are largely still struggling to procure even the most basic goods. The economy still remains in freefall and the international community is split between recognizing Maduro or Guiadó as the legitimate leader of Venezuela.

Prices are now doubling approximately every 19 days and thousands of Venezuelans are leaving the country each day. Protests are still widespread in Caracas and elsewhere and the United Nations has declared a migrant crisis in Venezuela and it has been said that there is "no end in sight to the massive movement of Venezuelan migrants and refugees."

One can only hope that, for the Venezuelan people, stability will occur soon and people in Venezuela will experience a return to the progress they knew at the height of their oil production and exportation. Unfortunately, there are few indicators of that return happening anytime soon while Maduro and Guiadó continue to jockey for power amongst an ever-worsening economy.

CPSIA information can be obtained
at www.ICGtesting.com
Printed in the USA
BVHW041716241022
650149BV00003B/230